Why Are the Casseroles Always Tuna?

A Loving Look
At the Lighter
Side of Grief

By DARCIE D. SIMS

Big A & Company
Albuquerque, New Mexico

Library of Congress Catalog Card number 90-82575
ISBN: 0-9618995-1-4
(previous ISBN: 0-9627165-0-2

To my mother, father and family,
who have always given me what I needed . . .
love, in endless supply

ABOUT THE AUTHOR

Darcie D. Sims

Darcie D. Sims is a psychotherapist and a grief-management specialist. She's also a wife and mom, a gypsy, a dreamer and a champion cookie baker. She developed "Psych-In-The-Box," a spoof on counseling drawn from the world of fast-food drive-up windows; and she invented the "Smile-On-A-Stick," which you will read more about in this book. In addition, she does wonderful things with tuna. Mostly, she roams the country trying to find a job, her niche in the world and a home with her husband Tony.

A bereaved parent, Darcie writes extensively in the areas of illness adaptation, grief management and coping creatively with the unexpected. Darcie is a collector of interesting stuff and she looks for the unusual, the unique and the *real* in people and in life.

Whenever her road gets rocky, she dons a pair of "rose-colored glasses." She has shared her sense of humor and her grief perspectives with people all over the world.

In 1976, Darcie and Tony's son, Austin, died of a brain tumor. Her life has not been particularly easy, but it has been interesting. In addition to her husband and her daughter, Allie, she is partial to sunshine, rainbows and Oreos. She has done a lot already, but she has more to do. While she keeps two pink flamingos in her yard, a rainbow on her shower curtain and a smile handy at all times, she is also learning to tap dance.

The struggle with Austin's illness and the process of survival have been enhanced by Darcie's highly developed sense of humor, which she freely shares with others. She has helped thousands of people find the laughter they thought they had lost forever when their loved one died.

Why Are the Casseroles Always Tuna? is her first published book, though there are over 400 manuscripts in her closet. She is hoping to bring another closet treasure to press within the year. She writes a regular column in *BEREAVEMENT* magazine and she does the laundry on Tuesdays.

Tuna has not been on the menu for years, but there's always a tuna casserole in the freezer—just in case.

ACKNOWLEDGMENTS

Dreams are fragile things. Most of the time they vanish in the reality of daylight or they are lost in the crowd of good intentions.

But, once in awhile, everything falls into place-the moon is in the right phase, the cookie jar is full and a dream becomes a reality.

"Thank you" isn't big enough for these fellow dreamers who helped change my fantasy into reality.

How do you say, "Thanks for the music"? A hug and love in endless supply to these members of the band:

Andrea Gambill, Editor, Bereavement Magazine

Paul Gray, Illustrator

Jonathan D. Dailey, Layout & Laughter

and the entire staff of Big A & Company and Creative Designs, Inc.

. . . and an extra, special hug and thank you to Tony and Allie— the magic in my life!

ABOUT ILLUSTRATOR PAUL GRAY

Paul Gray, to those who know him, is a minister (ordained for thirty-five years), a friend and an artist. During a lifetime of studying, serving and loving others, Paul has developed remarkable insights into the joys and sadnesses which are part of human life.

This insight, combined with genuine artistic talent, has allowed Paul to contribute to various care-oriented publications including BEREAVEMENT magazine.

Throughout this book, Paul's keen eye and practiced hand bring to visual life the thoughts and words of author Darcie D. Sims.

CONTENTS

INTRODUCTION

Why are the casseroles always tuna? Why is food the universal symbol of love, caring, concern and support?

The number of casserole dishes lined up on the counter chronicle the tragedies of our lives. Small crises are greeted with cookies, brownies and an occasional cake. Real emergencies bring forth soups, homemade breads and desserts.

Death, however, calls out the culinary talents of everyone who ever knew the deceased or the family, and the parade of food begins. Casseroles, meats, sandwiches, cakes, pies and cookies flow into the shaking arms of those whose lives have been forever changed in the blink of an eye or the sigh of a single breath.

I am eternally grateful for all that food! In the hours soon after death, when all reason has left, food provides a known and comforting activity. No one has to decide what to prepare or what to eat. One simply enters the kitchen and grazes . . . nibbling from each plate, tray and neatly wrapped foil-covered dish.

As the hours wear on, revealing new and painful realities, enough nourishment for an army continues to arrive. But along with the banquet comes an out pouring of love and comfort from family and friends.

No words are needed in those early hours, and few are offered that can match the true comfort of a warm brownie. One eats because it is a safe and familiar activity. In a world where everything else has changed, food and the people who deliver it provide an anchor, a rock on which to lean, a gift of the heart. When words fail, there is always chocolate.

Often we send food because we don't know what else to do or say. And I thank everyone who arrived at our home, that long ago day, laden with food and love. Those who came brought love and hope with them. I have no idea what anyone said to me in those early hours and days following the death of our son, Austin, but to this day, I remember who brought what!

I cherish the memory of the brownies and the cookies, and I can still see the row of casseroles lined up on the counter. . .tuna must have been on sale that week! Those plates of love are the reason for this small offering of thanks. This book is really a thank-you to everyone who loved us enough to overcome their fear of what to say and simply showed up.

This book is a collection of thoughts about the needs of the grieving. This collection of columns from *BEREAVEMENT* magazine has become a book—a thank-you for those who taught me it matters less what you say than that you say something. In times of hurt and pain and crisis, it matters that you come. Words are not the comfort that you bring—your presence is the healing gift.

Say whatever you wish, but bring brownies or a pie or a casserole. It would be nice if it weren't tuna, but don't let your tuna-filled cupboard stop you. Go! The simple gift of love, wrapped in a napkin or encased in a casserole, will speak more than you will ever know.

I also want to thank those who shared their joy with me, especially in those early days when I was sure there would never be another sunny day. Along with the tuna casseroles, there were bits and pieces of memories of our family before death intruded. The talk would turn to reminiscing, and the occasional smile that danced across my mind gave me hope and energy to face my journey through "The Valley."

This book is intended as a tribute to all the people who helped restore my sense of perspective and who taught me to search for joy— every day even in those days when winter seemed endless.

This is a lighter look at the most serious and painful journey that any of us will make; because as I learned that my progress is measured in inches, not miles, I also learned that how I crawl, walk or run those inches is up to me. No one can make the journey through the valley of the shadow of death for me, and no one can make it any less painful. I can, however, choose how I pick my next step....

Our son lived his life with laughter and love and joy—every day. I can do no less in his memory. I choose joy and laughter as a celebration that he lived. That has made all the difference.

Someone we loved has died, but the love and life we shared can never be forgotten.

May your footsteps be lighter and your journey be blessed with love in endless supply, an occasional tuna casserole and laughter . . . the most beautiful memory of all.

Christmas Is the Hardest Holiday!

Why is Christmas the hardest holiday? Is it because of all those traditions that meant so much before but now lie broken and empty in my heart? Is it especially hard now because every time I try to roll out the cookie dough, tears drop into little salt pools on the counter?

Is Christmas so hard now because of all the tinsel and tissue or because of all the crowds dashing madly into and out of stores, buying something wonderful for someone wonderful? Is Christmas so hard now because I don't need to shop or bake or decorate anymore? Is Christmas so hard now because I don't have someone wonderful anymore?

It's been a long time since I endured my first bereaved holiday season. But my heart sometimes still echoes with emptiness as I roll out the cookie dough or hang his special ornament on our treasure tree. I think that hurt will always be with me, but now I know it only as a momentary ache — not like the first year when grief washed over me in waves, each new wave hurling me deeper and deeper into despair.

And it's not like the second year's hurt when I found myself both surprised and angry that *it* hadn't gone away yet. I grew anxious about my sanity in the third year when my hands shook as I unwrapped the precious ornaments. When was I going to get better?! When was grief going to end?! Was I doomed to suffer miserably at every holiday for the rest of my life?!

The year the little satin balls fell off the tree, I gave up. Even the Christmas tree had died! As my daughter and I dragged the brittle (and shedding) mess out into the snowdrift on Christmas morning, I knew we had reached the bottom.

He had died, but we were alive. Had our grief so permeated our house, our lives, that even a Christmas tree could not survive? His death was more than enough . . . had we lost love, too?

That was the year we began to understand. And that was the year we decided to keep Christmas anyway. So what if our now completely bare tree was stuck in the snowdrift, already waiting for the garbage men? So what if the cookies were still a bit too salty with tears?

So in the middle of that Christmas day, now years past, we returned to that forlorn, frozen stick of a tree; and carefully, we decorated the bare branches with popcorn strings and suet balls (not quite the same as satin!). I'm sure we were a strange sight that afternoon, but with a mixture of tears and snowflakes, we began to let the hurt out and made room for the healing to begin.

With each kernel we strung, we found ourselves remembering. Some memories came with pain. Others began to grow within us, warming heart-places we though had frozen long ago. By the time we were finished, we were exhausted. Memories take a lot of work! At least we had a tree (though it was not the one we were expecting); but we had one, decorated with tears and memories, sadness and remembered laughter.

And now we've grown older (and maybe a little wiser) and we've learned that love isn't something you toss out, bury, pack away or forget. Love isn't something that ends with death. Life can become good and whole and complete once again . . . not when we try to fill up the empty spaces left by loved ones no longer within hug's reach, but when we realize that love creates new spaces in the heart and expands the spirit and deepens the joy of simply being alive.

We saved a tiny twig from that frozen tree . . . to remind us of what we almost lost. That was the year we chose to let Christmas come back. Now we don't have to wait for joy to return. For now we know it lives within us - - where Christmas is every day.

Why Are the Casseroles Always Tuna?

Why are the casseroles always tuna? Within hours of our son's death, our kitchen counter was overflowing with food. There were platters of sandwiches (could I freeze those for school lunches?), pots of soup, several pans of brownies and, by actual count, nine casseroles—eight of which were tuna.

People came to our door laden with food and advice. Along with the tuna, there were abundant suggestions: "Move immediately; don't touch a thing, Deary; call the insurance company;" and/or "Trust in God's will."

Tucked in with the cookies were words of wisdom that somehow left me cold and hungry for chocolate— that universal comfort food. We even got some rolls wrapped in a cloth napkin that had the Lord's Prayer stitched on it. (To tell the truth, all I wanted to do right then was tell God what He could do with His buns!

Fortunately, that feeling passed quickly, and I kept my mouth shut!) We had tuna with mushrooms, tuna with chips, tuna with noodles, tuna with black olives and tuna with peas (the little pale, canned ones). Gads! Did we have to be bereaved at mealtime, too!

Of course, we all know that a tuna casserole is the all-time, number-one choice of the "Let's-take-something-over-to-that-poor-grief-stricken-family—they'll-appreciate-it-at-a-time-like-this" folks. I know we ought to be grateful, but grieving is difficult enough—without tuna!

Tuna is versatile, however, and it can be disguised in many ways. It can be used as an exotic hors d'oeuvre for your next cocktail party; or you can stash it in the back of the refrigerator and hope it will either turn into something else, or that someone will think it is something else and eat it for a midnight snack.

You can freeze it and be the first one on your block to appear at the kitchen door of another friend in need. (Some of the casseroles that sat on my kitchen counter had obviously been around a loooooooong time!)

Bringing food is a universal symbol of caring and concern; but bring peanut butter, cheese and crackers, soup or Oreos— second only to chocolate as comfort food. Deliver dessert, a pitcher of orange juice, a basket of fruit or paper goods. (Napkins, paper plates and toilet paper are always welcome and needed, and a continuous roll of TP is much more practical for a grieving person than a pop-up box of tissues.)

So, dash to your kitchen and prepare something special to take to the family who is hurting, but leave the tuna on the kitchen shelf. Take something warm and comfortable: like chocolate-chip cookies or Pheasant Under Glass. Grief isn't ordinary, why should food be?

Wrap your gift with caring and bring it with simple silence and a gentle hug—leave the tuna, and the words of advice, at home—all we really need is something to eat and someone to listen.

And don't forget us three months from now. By then, both the cupboards and the heart are empty, and a knock at the kitchen door would sound lovely. Come by six months later, too. Maybe then even tuna would look good!

Looking for Joy

Do you know how long it took me to allow laughter and joy to return to my life? Do you know how far it has been from my side of this page to your side? Do you know how difficult it is to sit at my typewriter and think of anything funny (humorous is a more dignified word) about death?

It was a ten-year journey. It took me ten years to get from my side of this page to yours. A whole decade. Actually, it seemed more like a whole lifetime!

I liked my other life. In fact, I loved it! *BEREAVEMENT* was not the kind of magazine I had in the bathroom or on the coffee table! I was more of a Family Circle or Humpty Dumpty person. I never intended to write a book about grief. But then a single moment changed everything—and here I am.

Fourteen years ago, our son, Austin Van Sims, slipped away from his mom and dad and big sister. At peace, after a lifelong battle with a malignant brain tumor, he took with him all the hopes and dreams we had of being "an average American family."

We had only two children so that no one would have to share the window or ride on the hump in the middle of the back seat. We had two children because I had hundreds of recipes that served four. We had two children because we couldn't figure out how to have 1.6 children, which was the national average.

But something happened along the way to that dream, and in the flicker of a moment not only were our dreams lost, but the sounds of joy and laughter left our lives as well— perhaps as they seem to have left yours....

We now know the quietness that comes when we realize we are the only source of sound in our house. Like you, we know that loss—that emptiness—that brings us here to these pages in search of something to ease the pain; in search of something to stop the tears; in search of something to dream about again.

Right now, I can't think of anything else I'd rather be doing than living. But that wasn't always true, especially right after Austin's death when there were some days all I could think about was dying—either to join him or to relieve my pain. But I lived through that by grasping every day and claiming it as my own.

One day, each of us will rediscover whatever we cherish about life. Each of us will find the laughter that echoed throughout our life with our loved one—if we will look for it.

I'm here, on this side of the page, not to tell you how to be happy, but to tell you that you deserve to be happy again. I'd like to share with you how I did it; how I got to my own here and now. It took a lot of healing-time and a commitment to rediscovering the joy of living.

It's a different kind of joy, though. It's a happiness that's been robbed of its innocence and forged by a flame that has the power, if allowed, to destroy everything in its path.

But we don't have to dwell in the darkness forever.

11

Instead, we can choose to understand that our loved one's death was but a moment—a split second—of horror. When we can focus our remembrances on our loved one's life, it is possible that we can begin to understand that joy can return and even be comfortable.

We cannot find words to soothe the hurt. There simply aren't any! We cannot shield ourselves from the twists and turns of living. We cannot protect ourselves from experiencing life.

We can, however, build supports and safety nets. We can create cushions and pockets of comfort—places where we can rest momentarily, gathering strength to re-enter the crashing tides.

We can learn to smile again, maybe even return laughter to our lives. Cry all you want, but remember to laugh when you can, too. Your life with your loved one was filled with moments of laughter. Remember them; enjoy them again and again. Between the tears, allow the joy to return.

These pages will not try to bring you funny stories or irreverent jokes, but rather a message with a chuckle, a hope for returning joy, a gift of remembrance, a love letter of laughter.

Insist on joyfulness and a little silliness being a part of each day. Sometimes we cannot wait for fun and joy to be presented to us. We must make it happen!

What the world needs now is a paper airplane that carries our message of love and hope and laughter to friends, family— to everyone!

Become a pioneer right now and run your own flying circus. Follow the directions given here and make your own "Happy Planes" to send anywhere. Send one to your mother who is trying to understand (or just trying). Send one to your best friend who hasn't spoken to you since the funeral or to the neighbor who didn't bring a tuna casserole. (Bless her!) Send one to a child who needs some fun, and even send one to yourself, just because!

Mentally, verbally and physically sail these messages through the air. You could fold the paper airplane right now and let the joy of your loved one's life begin to replace the hurt and anger of death.

DIRECTIONS FOR "HAPPY PLANE"

Fold number 1, first; number 2, second; you figure it out from there.

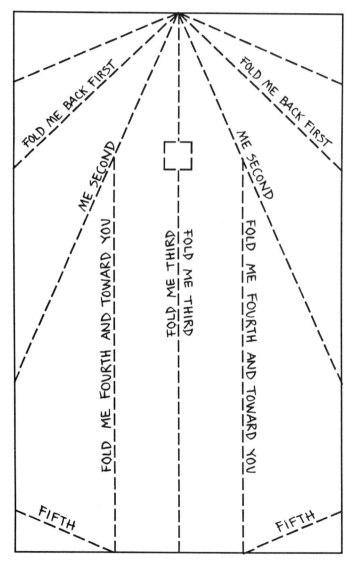

Spring Cleaning

For awhile, we lived in a town house: one of those creations designed to minimize house-keeping chores, mortgage payments and the tendency to accumulate more things than one needs to cross the Sahara in summer.

We moved into our town house because we liked the idea of no yard work, and we would not be burdened by comments like, "It's Saturday so mow the lawn." And since I hate housework, and it hates me back, we wanted a less-complex lifestyle.

Smaller places do have a certain appeal . . . especially during the "It's-Spring-and-that-means-let's-get-organized-around-here-and-throw-out-all-YOUR-stuff" mood that tends to permeate the months of March and April.

When you have only one closet, cleaning it takes a minimum of time. Opening the door starts the process, and if you are clever, you will be ready with a trash bag as you pry open the door. Be sure to do this at 2 a.m. when the other occupants in your town house are asleep; or during those few quiet moments of solitude you get after announcing that Dairy Queen is having a twenty-minute-only-special, and you have (thoughtfully) placed the keys in the car...

"Spring cleaning" is a phrase some psychologists have associated with grief in an effort to help patients rid their psyches of old memories, useless information and general clutter. Though it can be a painful process, it is this sifting and sorting that tells us, and the rest of the world, who we are (or were).

There are as many ways to Spring clean as there are homes and hearts and minds and spirits that need "adjusting" (a real psychological term thrown in just to remind me that I am a professional, too!)

How many times have you been told, "It's time to move on now" or, "It's time to get back to normal, " or "You mean you haven't gotten rid of *that* yet?" *That* can refer to a multitude of things, such as his favorite pipe or her torn bathrobe (attacked by the puppy during play). It could also be an odd assortment of baseball cards, used gum wrappers and dirty socks that were secreted under the bed—and left behind for you to find and cry over.

How come everybody else knows when it is time for me to Spring clean?! How come everybody else knows when it is time for me to open that closet and sort through all those memories, trying to decide which ones to keep and which ones to pass on to the Salvation Army? How come everybody else knows when it is time for me to get back to living?

I *am* Spring cleaning. I am sifting through all the stuff that made up my loved one's life, and I am learning to let go of a few things—slowly.

We moved to a town house so life wouldn't be so complicated. So I wouldn't have to go out into the yard and remember how wonderful it was to enjoy the first Spring flowers—with him. I don't want to cut the grass because we loved playing in it together, tickling our bare toes and laughing our way right through Spring and on into Summer.

We moved to a town house so we wouldn't be able to keep everything forever. (It doesn't stay around anyway, so why have storage space?) Why should we have cupboards that no longer need to hold the cereal that turns the milk pink, or closets that no longer need to hold baseball shoes, bats and crumpled homework pages? Why should we make room for memories? Why? Because, we can't live without them!

Spring is the time for Spring cleaning—for sifting and sorting and re-reading and remembering.

Spring is a time for some things to go and some things to stay. We just have to decide which ones do what. Spring is a time for renewal; when the earth begins to defrost after a harsh and bitter Winter.

It doesn't matter what time of year your loved one died. What does matter is that you begin to let Spring come back into your life. It does matter that you can finally open that closet and let the memories come out, along with the hurts and the hopes that you buried, too.

You never know what you're going to find when you start Spring cleaning. You might discover treasures you have long forgotten, or the tax papers you needed, or the Easter egg no one found last year. You might even find a few bits of joy lurking under the bed. (We found dust bunnies.)

What fun to recall how that stuff got there, or who might have been hiding under the bed when you were looking for volunteers for trash patrol!

Spring cleaning—a tradition that follows the footprints across your freshly waxed floor. I wish there were still footprints to clean up; but since there aren't, I'll just have to spend a few extra moments with the box of treasures I found. No time like the present to inspect all the stuff in search of a few bits of joy.

We lived in a town house for awhile, and it was then that I started a little patch of grass out front, planted a seed or two in a clay pot on the patio, and lived with what we had. Eventually, as we stretched out into something a bit larger, I found my heart was growing, too.

A Tribute to Mothers

May is the month we honor our mothers. Mothers are the source of worldly wisdom, dating advice, recipes and . . . underwear.

From the moment you were born, underwear was on your mother's mind. Worrying about undergarments was part of the nine-month training program our mothers endured before we arrived. Depending on how old you are now, your mother either spent a great deal of time hemming flour sacks or she invested a goodly portion of her retirement fund for Huggies by the ton. But, regardless of the decade, mothers and underwear are synonymous!

By the time we were out of diapers, our mothers had developed new concerns regarding our inner attire. It suddenly became terribly important to have training pants. Little boys got miniature versions of Dad's boxers or Jockey shorts, and daughters wore little white cotton numbers, sprinkled with tiny rosebuds or daisies. (I always suspected there were advantages to being a girl!)

Adolescence brought new fears to our mothers. Never mind worrying about the kid driving, dating or flunking math. Mothers worry about underwear! Somewhere on the winds of time float the universal words of all mothers: "Don't forget to change your underwear. You wouldn't want to be in an accident . . . What if you had to go to the hospital?"

My mother was also particularly fond of, "You're not wearing those are you?" (I used to believe my mother really did have X-ray eyes. How could she tell that I was wearing the black, Saturday bikinis on Tuesday?)

Mothers are so special, but how do you live with one? It isn't easy. It's even more difficult to live with a bereaved mom. So I'd like to share a few tips for living with a bereaved mother:

- Logic is a wondrous thing. It has built entire civilizations, put a man on the moon and given us television and fax machines. Logic can work with just about anything except politics and mothers! You probably have a better chance of persuading Congress than you do your mother. Mothers usually are not logical even under the best of circumstances, so don't imagine you can use logic to communicate with a bereaved mom. Custer had better odds!

- Bereaved mothers are often confused and unable to function at mealtimes, so when (and if) she serves tuna, refrain from asking, "Who died?" Some say grief lasts forever. So does tuna!

- When your mother forgets your name and starts running down her mental list of "whoever you are," try to be patient. By the time she remembers your name, she'll probably have forgotten what you were supposed to do!

- Except when it comes to garbage. Mothers never forget garbage. Just give up and take it out. Even a bereaved mother remembers garbage!

• The number-one disease in America is guilt. If you don't already have it, get some! Your mother has plenty, and she is always willing to spread it around. It doesn't matter what you have done or haven't done, she's a good mother and she's always willing to pass along some guilt.

Every day begins with the lunch box at the door, a kiss and a little guilt. "Did you feed the starving fish?" she asks. "Did you make the bed so your poor mother doesn't have to break her aching back?" Or, "Did you brush, floss and flush?" And the clincher: "Don't get hurt or into trouble!" Now you're doomed. If you do get hurt or into trouble (or both), your mother will *suffer.* She's guilty because she couldn't protect you from harm or trouble, and you're guilty because you did it to her! And you probably didn't wear the right underwear either!

Mothers! Without them, we wouldn't even be! They've given us so much: love, support, courage, graham crackers, underwear, even life itself. They have held our aching hearts and taught us that love is a living thing; not something to be buried and only remembered.

Their tears and love have raised us up tall and straight. Their hopes and dreams have lived on in us. If only we could adequately say, "Thanks. " If only we had said it a hundred times a day—every day! If only....

So, today, I'll stop the merry-go-round and pause to hug a daffodil, kiss a child and smile a rainbow—all in tribute to mothers.

Her love gave me life, and even if I had never known her or could barely remember her face or grasp her hand, I'd stop for awhile and remember to say "please" and "thank you."

Thanks, Mom, for love . . . and for the underwear!

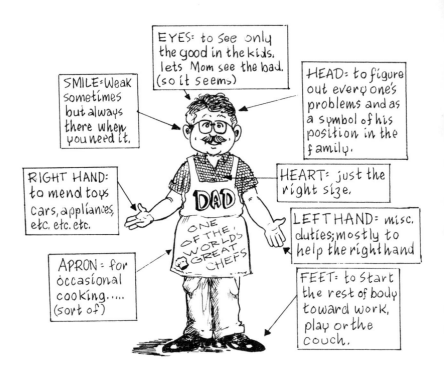

EYES: to see only the good in the kids, lets Mom see the bad. (so it seems)

SMILE=Weak sometimes but always there when you need it.

HEAD= to figure out everyone's problems and as a symbol of his position in the family.

RIGHT HAND: to mend toys cars, appliances, etc. etc. etc.

HEART= just the right size.

LEFT HAND= misc. duties; mostly to help the right hand

APRON = for occasional cooking..... (sort of)

FEET= to start the rest of body toward work, play or the couch.

DAD

ONE OF THE WORLDS GREAT CHEFS

Life With Father

Everything I know about barbecuing I learned from my dad. Every Saturday afternoon, my father began a ritual that eventually led to the family gathering around the medicine cabinet.

My dad is the only man I know who can take a perfectly wonderful piece of meat and turn it into fish. After my father would pronounce the meat "done," my mother would quietly open a can of salmon or defrost a tuna casserole, and we'd mark down in the family medical records another Saturday backyard barbecue. I love my dad dearly, but not his barbecuing!

Not everyone can be a dad, but everyone has a dad. Whether your dad is still out mowing the lawn or has already gone to the Hardware Store in the Sky, most of us have memories of our "Life With Father."

Over the years, our family has developed a number of rules about our dad. These have helped us coexist with the Great Barbecuer. Living with Dad had become a challenge, one which we still remember....

Dads are brave. Dads always enter the house first to check for burglars (and to get to the bathroom ahead of the rest of us). Dads check under beds and in closets before turning out your light at night, making sure no boogeyman is hiding anywhere. Dads climb on roofs to fetch stray kittens and kites, and dads loan their car keys to newly licensed sons and daughters. Dads are brave!

Dads sit at the head of the table. They sit there because they are the head of the family (as opposed to being the tail of the family, which is usually reserved for the last one in the family). Dads become head of the family because they have learned to carve the turkey. They take the lead in family discussions and they dispense "When-I-was-a-child" stories whenever things threaten to get out of control. Dads never let things get out of control, though, because mothers won't let them .

Dads are strong—or think they are. Our job is to help them believe this even if it means loosening the jar lid before giving it to them to open. Because dads are strong, they don't cry in front of us much. Some dads hide their pain in bottles, some in gruff words, some in stony silence. But dads are strong—at least on the outside.

Dads are busy. Most dads go to work every day. Some go every other day or every other month or every other year. Some already went to work, and some don't have any work to go to. But dads are very busy trying to figure out the mysteries of the universe so they can explain them to us. Dads know they must try to have the answers to all our "Why?" questions, even the hard ones—even the ones about death.

Dads can fix anything. They can fix leaky faucets, sometimes turning them into waterfalls. They save junk so they can turn it into "something useful someday." (Look what they did with us!) Dads mend fences, bicycles, dented fenders and broken hearts. They tell terrible jokes, make gigantic messes and wonderful sandwiches. Dads are the reason we are here. Without them we wouldn't be. So while some are still barbecuing with their dads on Saturdays, some are left with only warm and wonderful memories; some have other memories and some never knew their dads.

But, regardless of "life with father," our lives have been shaped by that man who, if only for a single moment, loved us enough to give us life.

My dad is a terrible barbecuer, but he still fixes my sink and listens to my aching heart. His strong arms surround me with love and his tears blend with mine as we struggle to find the "Why?" of change and the reasons for death. He is as puzzled as I am and just as helpless. He taught me to look at the stars and walk in the direction of their light, even if I don't know where I am going.

I think I'll call my dad this weekend and maybe we'll talk. Maybe we'll just look through the scrapbook and remember. Maybe I'll just chat with him in my heart. Maybe we'll cry and maybe I'll fire up the barbecue.

I wonder if Mom still has some tuna....

The Good Grief Diet

Though grief is a normal and natural reaction to loss, we sometimes experience confusing feelings. Grieving may cause physical and behavioral changes such as sleep irregularities or changes in appetite. (I, however, have never been able to say, "I'm so upset I can't eat a thing!")

We may also experience gastrointestinal disturbances (the clinical term for upset tummy), restlessness, spontaneous crying, irritability, sighing and muscle tension. There are about 10,000 other "symptoms" of grief as well, but we'll save those for another time.

Because so many of us experience our grief in our tummy, I would like to share my version of a popular stress diet with you. As always, check with your medical adviser (Reader's Digest or your bridge club) before staying on this "diet" for more than several years. Some substitutions are allowed, but only if you promise not to tell.

The Good Grief Diet

BREAKFAST

Sleep in.

(Grief makes us extra tired, so skip this meal and snuggle back under the covers. You'll have to get up eventually anyway to go to the bathroom and you can start the diet then.)

MID-MORNING SNACK

1/2 grapefruit.

(The other half was eaten by the hungry and angry crowd who appeared at your bedside several hours ago, demanding to be fed.)

1 piece whole-wheat toast, dry.

(Unless you have kumquat jam which is so tart that puckering uses up all the calories.)

8 ounces fruit juice.

(The milk carton was carefully replaced in the fridge, but it was empty.)

LUNCH

2 oz. turkey breast. (This menu is only for those who cannot get a friend to take them out to lunch.)

1 small crab leg. *(I like crab better than frog . . .)*

6 cups zucchini, steamed. *(I know this seems like a lot of zucchini but if you eat less than 6 cups, there will only be more zucchini for later. It keeps growing!)*

32 oz. herb tea. *(You must drink 64 oz. of fluid a day, and you are already behind!)*

1 fudge-nut brownie. *(The comfort foods are required.)*
OR 1 Oreo cookie
OR 1 serving chocolate mousse.

LATE-AFTERNOON SNACK

6-pack diet soda *(If you **run** after the ice-cream
3 Fudgesicles and truck, you may have an extra
a Nutty Buddy Nutty Buddy or half an ice-cream
sandwich.)*

DINNER

Go out. Grief has robbed you of any creativity or pleasure in the kitchen.

LATE-NIGHT SNACK

Entire double fudge chocolate cake, OR one 16-inch chef special pizza, OR BOTH!

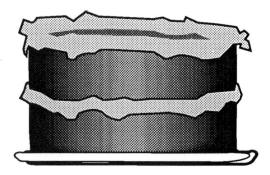

Diet Rules

- Tasting has no calories.

- Foods used for medicinal reasons contain no calories. (Examples are foods consumed for "comfort": Oreos, cheesecake, hot chocolate.)

- Foods eaten in the dark don't count.

- If no one sees you eat, you didn't.

- Eating celery burns up more calories than it contains. Therefore, eating a minimum of twenty-five sticks a day will cause a surplus of energy which can be used to "balance" the hot-fudge sundae binges.

- Broken pieces of food do not count. The process of breaking causes "calorie leakage." Break all cookies before eating.

- Foods consumed at the movies or while bowling don't count on your daily total because they are considered to be a part of the entertainment package rather than body fuel.

- Sobbing while eating causes calories to float away. It also releases tension, which allows one to enjoy more food later.

- Eating your loved one's favorite food is always "legal."

Love doesn't have calories!

We Didn't Move This Summer

After much serious deliberation, careful weighing of the pros and cons and, finally, flipping a coin, we decided not to move this summer. We decided to make our stand right where we were—to build our castles, treasure our memories and grow old in familiar places. It was settled. We would not move.

I was glad we wouldn't have to deal with realtors, struggle with packing boxes and take on the United States Postal Service. Moving is for brave souls who hear the whisper of distant winds, who dream of untamed waters, who seek romance, fame, adventure. Moving offers escape, change and challenge.

Moving also offers crises, lost luggage and instant insanity. I was really glad we decided not to move!

But the job offer (for me) and the military orders (for my husband) arrived on the same day....

Living with a FOR SALE sign is not for the frail, and an "Open House" notice can cause heart failure.

No one was allowed to use their bed, closet or bathroom as long as that sign was up.

When the negotiations were finally completed, we all breathed a bit easier.

Now, packing became a challenge. Dad was going in one direction (dictated by the United States Army), and the rest of us set our sights on a new job and location for Mom.

Decisions were impossible. Who would get the blender? Does Dad really need the vacuum cleaner? How do you divide up the record albums? Who wants the iron? And what about the scrapbooks?

What about the memories? What about *his* stuff, so carefully packed away, neatly boxed and sealed against time, and labeled simply, "Big A"? Who would get the oh-so-few pictures? Surviving Big A's death had been hard enough. Moving was simply stirring up all those things we had so neatly packed away.

Moving tests the strength of the human spirit. How can one possibly begin to wade through all the treasures (rudely referred to by other members of the family as stuff) one accumulates over the years? The sorting and sifting and remembering took a heavy toll on all of us. "Do you need it?" became the byword. Later it became, "Do you REALLY need it?"—and still later, "Will you die without it?" Eventually, "There's room for either you OR it!"

Goodbyes were fun, at first. Mostly because they were delivered along with hors d'oeuvres, backyard barbecues or sinfully wonderful chocolate cakes. But it gradually became harder and harder to say, "goodbye."

Eventually, we'd part without saying goodbye. "It sounds so final." (It is.) "We'll see each other again...." (Probably, but not until a crisis sends us scurrying back home.)

Saying goodbye is a lot like grieving.

The last phone call. The last hug. The last glimpse of a waving hand in the rear view mirror....

Moving is like dying and not waking up in Heaven.

Dad left first. (I believe it is a military regulation that the military member not be involved with the actual packing-loading-unpacking process. Something to do with national security, I think.) Then the moving van came and left. The caravan headed east, looking more like a band of gypsies who had just robbed a Twinkies store than an orderly "relocation" (a term the realtor used frequently—especially when I kept insisting that we were not moving). Once we were actually on the road, adventure after adventure befell us. We discovered a new language as we tried to communicate rest room and food stops to each other via the CB radio. I think the entire world knew where the Sims ate, watered and slept!

We battled traffic, and road maps were often held upside down, making east where west was supposed to be. Every night I called Grandma and Grandpa to relate how thankful I was that we were not moving.

At our new location, we bought a house—complete with a lot of things I didn't order and missing many of the things I did—and we moved in. The lawn died (drought). We said a lot of hellos. My daughter mastered freeway driving—at rush hour. When Dad got settled, he discovered he had gotten the iron and the blender. We got most of his socks.

The scrapbooks had been divided and shared so we each could have something to help jog our memories when the emptiness of being in a new place steals in at night, and the rest of the world is pretending to be asleep.

Moving means beginnings and endings—all jumbled together. Moving is sorting and sifting and beginning again and again. So is grief. Maybe that's why we talk about "moving through grief."

We can survive grief just as we can survive moving, as long as we don't demand the new be the same as the old. I'll make it as long as I don't keep trying to dial the old phone number, or keep looking for the old me.

Can we survive? Yes, but only when we learn to bring a little something of yesterday with us—just a memento for comfort—without trying to re-create the castle where now stands a parking lot.

Bring a little something with you. Tuck it gently away near your heart. Then open that door and venture outside. There's a whole new place waiting to be known . . . as home.

The Perfect Costume

I've finally found the perfect Halloween costume! For years, it has been a struggle to think of a disguise that NO ONE ELSE would have. I've appeared as Cinderella, a bag lady, a witch and an odd assortment of whatever my mother had in her closet at the moment. (I never, however, went disguised as underwear or fruit!)

Halloween has always been my favorite holiday. It arrives just before the real frost sets in and, even if only for a few hours, allows everyone to return to the Land of Make-believe. It also heralds in the Holiday Season and marks the first classroom party where the room mothers get to strut their stuff!

For children, Halloween poses few problems—unless you count as one of childhood's true traumas the dilemma of how large-a-treat-bag to carry. It was a terrible decision! Should I take the plastic pumpkin Dad brought home from Woolworth's or should I take a pillowcase? (I always had BIG hopes!) Or would Mother's practicality win out, leaving me stuck with a plain, brown grocery bag again? It made for some difficult moments in my house.

But, as I grew older, the costume became the center of all my attentions; and by the time I was in college, weeks went into creating just the right effect. After I was married, it got even worse. One year, my husband and I were invited to a M.A.S.H. costume party. We were told to come either as a M.A.S.H. character or a favorite disease. Tony went as Klinger because we had an old ball gown that fit perfectly. I went as diarrhea.

That was a long time ago, and it has been an equally long time since I felt much like dressing up and playing pretend. The years between have not all been kind, and I have to admit that I have missed quite a few Trick-or-Treats. Mostly, I missed them because I couldn't think of anything to wear or anyone to be. The Land of Make-believe seemed non-existent, and being myself wasn't very funny.

I had lost Halloween. I had lost "Trick-or-Treat." I had lost fun. I felt I had been tricked, not treated, and nothing would pass my broken heart that could make me smile again . . . nothing.

Fall began to seem like a time of death. I counted fallen leaves. I noted bare tree limbs and frost on the dead grasses. I watched the daylight hours grow shorter and felt the winter creep inside where no Halloween could dare to live.

I even started giving out treats I hated . . . those icky, taffy things that stick to dental work or those popcorn balls that were on sale after Halloween last year. (I even considered handing out tuna balls....)

But the years kept coming, and every calendar still showed Halloween. As soon as I turned the page on Halloween, it was downhill toward Turkey Day and then the dreaded Christmas! Gads . . . would life never stop? Mine did a long time ago. Why didn't the calendar?

And then, several years ago, I found the perfect Halloween costume. (Unfortunately, it wasn't Halloween, but who could let a perfectly good costume go to waste?) I looked in the mirror one morning and announced to that wretched reflection that I was bereaved, and suddenly, my costume fit!

"Grief" can be the perfect all-occasion costume. It goes with everything, fits every size and needs no explanations. (Who would dare ask what being bereaved means?) Now, whenever I wear my bereaved costume, I know people *understand.* It's the all purpose costume and it assures you proper credit for your (ahem) strange behaviors.

Wearing "grief" is easy. Just look natural. After all, people expect you to be different—at least for a week or two. After that, you can just say, "I'm bereaved," and a hush will fall over the crowd. You can then wear your costume for as long as you wish. No one will challenge you (or your behaviors), except perhaps the little goblin who knocks at your door (or your heart) and asks for "trick or treat, please."

If a small child dressed as "Alf" can muster up a smile and a, "Thank you," as you drop in a handful of broccoli chips, then surely you can find the courage to accept what you've got and keep on knocking on life's doors.

Halloween lasts only one night. The Land of Make-believe lasts only a few moments. So, Cinderella or Prince Charming, reach out to the Fairy Godmother and take one more dance . . . the glass slipper was once yours. The memory of it can never be lost.

I'm bereaved, and so are you. But Halloween lasts only one night. Perhaps it is time to put down the mask, forgive the Trick and join the Treaters.

MENDED BY LOVE

A Family Circle

I saw my first holiday display this afternoon, and naturally I was immediately caught up in the spirit of the upcoming holiday season. Whipping out my charge card, I dashed madly through the aisles, humming Silver Bells and tossing item after item into my basket.

I had only gone into the store to buy grass seed, fertilizer, bulbs and sunscreen. But I soon discovered it was too late for that nonsense! Now it was time for The Holidays. I felt as if I had hardly had time to think much about Summer; and now, suddenly, I was expected to make ready for The Season.

As I sweated my way back to the parking lot, I began to wonder how I would get through another of these holidays. It's barely Fall, and I'm supposed to be ready. I'm not sure I'll every be ready! Will I always be buying grass seed and fertilizer when everyone else is thinking toys and ties and fruitcake?

How long will I dread the thought of stuffing a turkey? That could take forever, and since we still have a tuna casserole or two in the freezer....

Funny how I never noticed how loud tinsel can be as it dangles from the aisle markers—it echoes everything I no longer have. Fertilizer in my basket and an ache in my heart are out of place in the Land of the Blue Light Special. The ad says I'm supposed to be buying happiness.... Where do I find that?

Where is *that place,* that place where happiness begins again? Certainly one of the places is here— right in your hands— within these pages of hope and help, laughter and love. You and I, and all the others who have gotten through these pages, have shared a common experience together. We've laughed and cried together, and we have become a "family" of sorts.

By now, you know how I like Oreos and how I have a "meaningful relationship with tuna," and I know how you are hurting and reading and learning to survive. We are learning to walk together through "The Valley." We are a family.

Together, we will find that aisle marked "Happiness" and we will get ready for the holidays. Together, we shall join hearts and hands across the earth and decorate the world with hope and healing and remembered laughter. We shall remain forever linked through the love of our absent children, parents, husbands and wives, siblings, grandparents, friends— all of our loved ones who dance across the rainbows ahead of us.

We are a family circle—broken by death, mended by love!

For this holiday season, whether you are buying toys or ties or tuna: May this day, and every day, be days for us to laugh and sing, to dance and dream. May this day, and every day, be days of celebration and the chance to give one more hug, to say one more, "I love you."

May love be what you remember most.

Basements

January is depressing. It's a month of bitter cold, gloomy days and leftovers. It's a month of used Christmas bows (surely we should save them for next year) and things that don't fit. (Either they didn't fit before the holidays or they don't fit now!) January is also a month with too many days in it.

January is a letdown from the hustle and bustle of the holiday season. It is a month to "get through." January is a month to survive.

I've decided to spend January in my basement. After all, basements are often dark and gloomy (suits my mood), in need of organization (describes my life perfectly) and could use a good cleaning (similar to shaking the cobwebs out of my brain).

Therefore, I would like to have Hallmark declare January "Basement Month" and come out with a suitable card to help me celebrate my hibernation. That's where I am going to spend the icy, snowy month of January. I have all sorts of plans. I can tackle the still-packed boxes from our move last summer. I can arrange and re-arrange to my heart's content without annoying the rest of the family who dwell upstairs and who think that "everything looks fine, Mom." (They, however, think that Kmart on Exchange Day looks fine, too.)

I can sift through boxes of unknown treasures, sorting and tossing. I can count my blessings in the soft darkness of a basement lit with a single light bulb, and no one will see the tears that I hid so well during the holidays. I can come up one blessing short and gasp in the pain (always there, but not often brought out to light anymore), and then let it dissipate in the far reaches of the basement's gloom.

I think I will organize the basement according to the seasons: Spring, with the flower pots, fertilizer, garden seeds and bicycles. Summer, with the lawn mower, garden hoses and rubber rafts. Fall will have the rakes and the Halloween decorations. And Winter. Winter will have the snow shovels, snow boots, sleds, ice skates, skis (and crutches)—all stored neatly, side-by-side.

The holiday decorations will be stored halfway between Fall and Winter because of the great debate in our house about when is the proper time to put up the decorations. This debate is topped only by the one about when to take them down. So far, the earliest we have discarded the holiday decorations is Christmas afternoon, and Easter wins as the latest.

I will need to have another category in my basement, however. It will be the Fifth Season . . . the season of miscellaneous.That's where I'll stash everything that doesn't fit anyplace else—somewhat like my grief, which seems to pop up at the most inconvenient times.

I wish I could compartmentalize it, organize it, so I wouldn't be caught off guard. I wish I could put it away for a time—storing it in the recesses of my base-ment— knowing where it is when I need it. But grief doesn't work that way. My basement probably won't work that way either!

Grief is there, always. You don't "get over IT." You can't hide from IT. You can't put IT aside until it's convenient. In fact, the more you try to avoid IT, the more IT catches you. It's a bit like that mysterious gift you once got from some distant relative. The more you try to forget it, the more it stays. Grief is in all the seasons of your life.

But grief doesn't have to be a burden all the time. Like the things you have stored in the basement, it can be sifted through, re-organized and dealt with. It doesn't have to be stashed in the darkest corner of your heart.

Part of grief is learning to live without the person who made your life so incredibly wonderful. But the other side of grief is remembering how wonderful life can be and getting busy not just surviving, but living!

The snowflakes are still just as lovely and mysterious. The Spring flowers will bloom again, with their sweet message of LIFE. Summer will bring more warm evenings and fireflies to chase, and Fall will turn its leaves one more time.

Winter will come again and another January will be celebrated in the basement . . . not because it is the only place we can find solace and comfort, but because the sifting and sorting and reorganizing are an important part of our process.

Your life with your loved one was filled with moments of laughter. Remember those moments, enjoy them again and again. Don't just store them in the basement of your heart.

So, join me this month as I make good my one New Year's resolution. I resolve to keep my basement clean, organized and usable. It will NOT become a repository for castoffs and the no longer-useful in my life. It will be what it really is: a part of my house, my home, my life.

I will be in the basement this month, not escaping the snow (I love that!), but getting ready to heal.

The memories will always hurt, but there also will always be love, and you cannot discard, bury or lose the love you shared.

Let the joy of your loved one's life begin to take the place of the hurt and pain of his death.

Ode to the Shoebox

I came across the perfect shoebox yesterday. It was just the right size—not too big and not too small. The sides weren't caved in from having a pair of too-big shoes crammed into its depths and it still had a good top on it. It was the perfect box!

I could wrap it with red-and-white crepe paper and add a pretty bow, and everyone would know whose box it was. And there would be lots of Valentines to go in that box . . . so many it might even overflow. I hugged that box when I found it yesterday.

Too bad I found it now—thirty-five years too late! Oh well, sometimes that seems to be the story of my life—too late or too early or too small or too big or too something. Right now, too empty.

There are lots of uses for shoeboxes. I used to be so organized that I actually put shoes in them; but now they hold odd assortments of photos, trinkets, old sales receipts, canceled checks and a million of the "to do" lists that I make every January.

41

Shoeboxes are like little time capsules holding treasures (or trash) from the past. They lie buried beneath the long dresses in the back of the closet or stored on shelves that no one can reach, or they are jumbled into dark, secret places in the basement. There are lots of memories stashed away in shoeboxes.

Shoeboxes and Valentines are symbols of February. February seems sort of stuck in the calendar—a break from the post holiday gloom and a rehearsal for the rites of Spring (when we get new shoeboxes with new shoes in them).

No one buys shoeboxes. They are just there whenever you need them, bringing comfort and security and a peace of mind that we will always have enough room to store the mementos of the world as long as we have shoeboxes.

Shoeboxes are also the repository of those little dark brown fluted papers that spelled "guilty" whenever someone found them in the kitchen garbage. So, like all clever (and chocolate-loving) snitchers, we stored in a shoebox well hidden in the back of the closet, the incriminating evidence of our midnight raid on the box of Valentine chocolates.

Usually, I could remember to empty the box by Summer, but occasionally, I would find a stash of little candy papers sometime in October or November.

Ah, I loved my shoebox. I dreamed of bringing home a box overflowing with cards, ribbons, chocolates and those little sweetheart candies—the ones that said, "I LUV U" or "SWEETIE PIE" or "CUTIE." I used to spend all of the end of January anticipating Valentine's Day, looking for just the right shoebox, and picking out just the right boy.

Valentines haven't changed much over the years. The pictures and cartoon characters are different, and now the envelope size must meet postage regulations, but the messages are the same.

Actually, shoeboxes haven't changed that much either and I'm kind of glad. Everything else in my world has changed since then . . . since the days when dreams were free and the world seemed to be just waiting for me and my shoebox. So, I'm glad Valentines and shoeboxes are still around.

I've perfected my chocolate-poking technique now and I don't have to hide the fluted wrappers anymore. I'm glad LOVE hasn't gone out of fashion. It still comes wrapped in bright-pink foil and has icky-tasting envelopes. If I'm missing the sender of my special Valentine this year, I've still got my shoebox of memories and a couple of old candy wrappers to remind me of the love that sent my heart zinging!

"Once upon a time" isn't really so long ago and "forever" seems more manageable now, too. So, I wish you Happy Heart's Day.

You wouldn't be reading this if you had not loved someone at some time. The special day and the shoebox are still yours, so fill them with memories (and a chocolate or two), but don't stash the box away this time. Celebrate the love that never goes away!

Just Wondering

The memory winds of Spring came calling today.
Icicles melting. Ruts in the road.
I thought I was beginning to thaw....

And then you whispered across my mind,
And I remembered.
It was Winter again.

—D. Sims

How do the tulips know which way is up, especially when I couldn't remember last Fall when I just tossed them in the holes? Are some of them now poking through the other side of the world?

I've always wondered how the geese know when it's time to come home, and how they can remember exactly where home is? While I'm still having a hard time figuring out the freeway system in Kansas City, they're winging their way home across thousands of miles of unmarked air! Does that mean geese are smarter than I?

And why does the groundhog control the arrival of Spring? For anything that important it should at least be reported by something more elegant than a rodent with a fur coat—maybe a gazelle or a unicorn.

And why did it snow more in Alabama this year than it did in Iowa? Who is in charge of that?

Why is a baker's dozen thirteen? When it comes to chocolate doughnuts, even thirteen isn't enough.

Why does the sun still get me up every morning, especially when I have been quite specific about not leaving a wake-up call? Why is mud brown? If we are going to have a lot of it around, then why isn't it clear? I probably should just give up and install mud-colored carpets and kitchen tile. Some things are not worth fighting.

Why are income taxes due during the gentle month of April—just when everything in the world Is waking up and growing brand new? They might as well be due in January along with the colds, post-party depression and the blahs. Why waste such a lovely month on taxes?

Why do we whisper at funerals? Is it out of respect for the dead, or because we are afraid of waking someone up? My son lived his life at the top of his lungs, why shouldn't we say goodbye so at least he could hear us?

Why are some people thoughtful and why are some like those tulips I planted upside down? Some speak with their hearts and some without benefit of a brain. Why?

Why are there clouds to entertain little kids on warm May days when they still have to be inside behind a school desk? Why does it rain only on weekends?

Why are sales at the grocery store on Wednesday when my family is hungry for *that* on Tuesday?

Why does Winter come before Spring? Is it so we will fully comprehend the blessedness of rebirth after the quietness of the earth's deep sleep?

Why do we clear the land before we do the Spring planting? Can't the roots go around the rocks like I have to? No one seems to be clearing my path—yet the roots hold fast. Why am I still growing when I once thought (and maybe wished) that I had died? Why does the day keep turning into night, and then into day again and again and again?

Why is Spring the time for some things to go and some things to stay, for the snow to melt and the earth to stretch? Why do weeds grow faster and stronger than the tender vegetables in my garden? Why do the squirrels beat me to the best apples, and why do bees buzz the most fragrant blooms—just as I bend to sniff?

Why is "Why?" such a hard question?

Why does the ice cream melt from the bottom up and drip through the cone? Why do they put the cherry on the top? I want another one—at the bottom!

Why do people die and where do they really go? Why do children ask, "Why?" all the time, and why do grownups grow impatient? Why do red M & M candies taste better than the other colors, and why do people fiddle with the Oreo middle?

And why do we have to know why all the time? Why can't we live with uncertainty, with not knowing, with the unexpected? Why do we have to always have labels and little signs that tell us what's in the cans on the shelf and what's planted in what row in the garden? Why can't we live with a little more sense of adventure and a little less need to always know. Why can't we let up a little on the "Wonder Whys?" and gamble a bit?

Why do I have to turn the page or answer the phone or open the door? Why can't I live with the mystery of not knowing for a little while?

Why do I continue to search for new beginnings when I liked the way it was, and why do I still hurt when it's been so long?

Why do I think these "whys," especially in the Spring? The rest of the world seems to be celebrating a reprieve from Winter. Why are parts of my heart still frozen?

Why?

Because....

FIRST
PLACE

MEAT LOAF

Memories of Mom's Meat Loaf

Though I have always loved my mother, I didn't fully appreciate her until I became one, too. I can remember her smile and the glee in her voice as she told me (more than a thousand times), "Wait until you have a child of your own. You'll see!" Well, Mom, now that I have a child of my own—now that I am a mom, too, I DO SEE! And what a sight it is!

I see the messes that I made, the Band-Aids that you dispensed, the mountains that we conquered and the reason for the rules that have been handed down through generations of mothers:

- DIRTY CLOTHES BELONG INSIDE THE HAMPER.
  For years, I believed we had a magic hamper in our house. I put the clothes in it, and they reappeared in my bureau drawers several days later—clean and ironed! It seemed miraculous.

When I was twelve, my mother introduced me to Mr. Washing Machine, Mr. Dryer (or Clothesline), and Mr. Iron. That was the end of the Magic Hamper myth. (I noted, with dismay, that my husband still believed in the Magic Hamper when we first got married.)

- SOCKS MUST HAVE MATES.
  These mates must match not only in color, but in size, as well. If I remembered to pair them up before depositing them in the Magic Hamper, I rolled them together. It seemed like a good idea at the time. My mother thought otherwise.

- CLOSETS HAVE A PURPOSE.
  So do drawers and shelves. My mother begged me to discover the wonders of drawers and closets. I did, but only when I had to share a dorm room with an impossibly messy person, and we couldn't find the ringing phone! I can only pray for my teenage daughter!

- THE LAST PERSON IN THE BATHROOM IS TO WIPE OUT THE SINK, CLOSE THE LID AND TURN THE FAUCET OFF ALL THE WAY.
  We have solved this challenge by having a bathroom for each person in our home, but I have noticed that I still have this rule. I've also added one that I think my mother was too polite to request. Dried toothpaste is to be removed from the sink weekly.

- WIPE YOUR FEET AT ALL TIMES WHEN ENTERING.

- FEED ALL PETS BEFORE FEEDING SELF.

- DO YOUR HOMEWORK (OR YOUR FATHER WILL HELP YOU).

- BEDS ARE FOR SLEEPING IN, NOT FOR JUMPING ON OR FOR STORING ALL WORLDLY POSSESSIONS UNDER. (REMEMBER THE CLOSET?)

48

- EAT WHATEVER IS ON YOUR PLATE—ALL OF IT. "Remember the starving children somewhere." I often wondered what the peas on my plate had to do with the starving (and lucky!) children somewhere who didn't have any peas.

These rules became a part of our family and they survived numerous family council meetings, changing social trends and several strikes on our part. I never knew how strong my mother was until I became one myself!

I never knew my mother's miracle meat-loaf recipe either. It remained a mystery for decades. Memories of that meat loaf lingered long after the well-worn meat-loaf pan found its way to the junk heap.

Memories of that meat loaf floated down through the years, always eluding me, always teasing me, always reminding me that I could not be a "proper mother" until I had mastered meat loaf.

It probably takes a lifetime to figure out the meat-loaf part of being a mother, like how to make it when you can't afford meat or how to make it stretch when there are too many around the table or how to make it when you are sick (and tired!). I'm working on it, Mom. Just like I'm working on being the kind of mother you have been to me: patient, kind, loving, brave and faithful.

Mom, how do I make meat loaf when there's an empty chair at the table and no one wants to eat? How do I make it taste like something expensive and elegant? How do I turn the ordinary into the wondrous? How did you make everything that way?

Meat loaf is one of the signs of motherhood, evidence of her creativity and love. This month, the month of motherhood, magic hampers, meat loaf and miracles, I lift my heart in celebration of your gift of life to me, and pass it on to the next generation of mothers.

I'm working on the meat loaf, Mom.

Dad

No one can fill my dad's shoes.

It's not that they're that big—we just can't find them! My dad gave up wearing shoes and suits and ties when he retired from a lifelong career in the U.S. Army. He favors soft moccasins and loose T-shirts now, and we can finally tell time the "civilian way." Supper is now at 6 p.m. instead of 1800 hours, and reveille is a distant memory.

I have lots of memories about my dad. Some I wish I could take back, and others are so cherished that tears still tickle the corners of my eyes. There are boxes and boxes of memories stashed away in the closet and mounted neatly in the scrapbooks, but still there aren't enough.

I wish we could have bronzed my dad's combat boots and put them on top of the TV set—like those baby shoes you always see in people's living rooms. Then we could remember Dad better. We'd have tangible proof that Dad was here. Why else do people spend that much money bronzing baby shoes? It's to capture the moment, to preserve the instant that those shoes were necessary, to prove to ourselves that once those shoes were needed, to remind us of a gentler time when things weren't so complicated.

My mom says she has plenty of memories and that a pair of bronzed combat boots on top of the TV would just be another thing to dust. She says she spent a lifetime dusting Dad and that she doesn't intend to do so anymore. She's "retired" too!

I have plenty of memories of Dad, but I think I want to bronze some of them so they don't wear out with time.

The drone of a thousand lawn mowers on a Saturday morning reminds me of Dad. I hear Dad every time we pass a Dairy Queen. He used to sneak an extra scoop of marshmallow topping and sometimes he'd plop one on my ice cream, too. I'd like to bronze that marshmallow plop.

I keep hearing the sounds of Dad everywhere. As I shut the window against the rain, I hear him reassuring me that the thunder is really only the elves bowling. I hear Dad reading stories of Winnie-the-Pooh, and even now, as I climb the stairs to my bed, I can hear his famous night time tales of Great, Great, Great Grandfather and how he settled the West!

I can still hear the footsteps of a thousand trips for bedtime water (we always demanded kitchen water, never bathroom water). Each step I take toward my own bed brings an echo of those wonderful sleepy moments, and I wish I could have them cast in bronze.

I can still hear him in the early morning, rattling around in the kitchen, trying not to wake anyone. I wish I could bronze those quiet snatches of hushed conversations Mom and Dad shared before the rest of us interrupted the day.

I think my sense of humor comes from Dad, and life with my father often was humorous. He taught me to laugh and to dream and to work; but he didn't laugh (not out loud anyway) when I wanted to be a professional baseball player, nor did he choke the summer I did ballet. I wish I could have bronzed that look!

He suffered through my algebra and what he referred to as "an endless procession of bums" that I kept bringing home. If only I could bronze the whispered, "I love you," as we walked down the aisle to my wedding.... I wish I could bronze the joy of Dad greeting his only granddaughter for the first time and his look of awe as he held her tiny hands, remembering my own once-tiny hand in his....

He wrote poetry and created magic with his words, yet he rarely shared his sorrows. I used to think dads didn't have any sadness, but now I know differently. Etched in my heart forever is the moment of goodbye between Dad and Son and between Grandpa and Grandson.

Etched, too, is the love that ties us together. I don't need to capture that in bronze and place it atop the TV in the living room so I won't forget that love really happened. It really did happen, and every time I hear a lawn mower or pass a Dairy Queen, it happens again and again. The magic still lives, and so does the laughter.

Grief has given me a new time frame. I measure things IN NOW, not next week or next month or next summer. I catch as many moments as I can.

Laugh a little, weep some, too, but whatever you do, celebrate the legacy of your dad. You are the moment of his love.

I love you, Dad.

Maybe it would be cheaper to bronze one of his moccasins....

The signs read: LAND of OUGHT · EXPECT · DON'T CRY · CRY ETC. ETC. · DON'T HURT · BE HAPPY

Running Away

I quit today. I gave up on the human rat race, un-plugged the coffee pot, put on my roller skates and ran away to join the circus. I had always wanted to join the circus; but even more than that, I had always wanted to run away.

I tried to run away once before when I was nine years old. I can't remember why anymore, but I do remember when I was sorting through my socks and underwear, my mother came in and helped me pack. (Running away was going to be more difficult than I had thought.) I couldn't leave my teddy bear and I had to have my "magic power ring" (remember Captain Midnight?) And I did need pajamas and a sweater.

After reaching the wise, nine-year-old decision to lighten my load by not taking any underwear, I tromped out of the house. I got as far as the corner when my dad leaned out of the car and offered me a ride to the bus station. How can you run away when everyone is helping you go?!

Well, today no one helped me go. I don't think anyone even knows I'm gone yet. But I've had it and I want to run away.

Maybe I can find that place where hurt doesn't live. Maybe if I don't get a phone (or at least have an unlisted number), pain won't find me. At least ringing phones won't be bringing me terrible messages I just don't want to answer anymore.

I don't want to be strong anymore, either. I'm tired of hearing "You're so strong. I don't know how you can do this. I'd die if it had happened to me!"

Yes, you probably believe you would die if this happened to you, except no one will even let you die! There are too many things to do and think about. *Too* many decisions to be made and too little help to make them. There is too much to do and too little energy.

Running away seems pretty OK with me, just like it did when I was nine. Except then, I ran out of sandwiches by the time Dad and I got to the bus station and I got lost on the way to the bathroom.

I wanted to run someplace where no one would know me; where no one would ask me anything; where no one would care about me or want me to be something or somebody I couldn't possibly be—but especially where no one would expect anything of me! I think I would have made it, too, except I couldn't decide where to go. Any place far away from where I hurt sounded OK to me.

That's why I wanted to run away then, and it's the reason I ran away today. Everyone EXPECTS something of me. Everyone has a time frame for me and chores for me to do, and everyone knows the way I OUGHT to feel and think and be!

Ought is the ugliest word in the human language. It is just a cover-up for expect. We "expect" this of you (like a clean room, neat homework and good grades—and later, a good job, a clean home, a well-balanced menu and on and on and on....)

I have come to expect things of others too, and worse yet, I expect things of myself! Often, things that start with the word ought end with disappointment and despair. I can't hold up the world any longer. I want to run away!

I think I ought to be happy by now . . . no matter how long "by now" is. I think I ought to be normal again (was I ever?) Everyone else thinks I ought to be busy again, filling my life with "something meaningful."

Even the world has some oughts for me. The books tell me I can "take as long as a year or two to put my life back together." Well, it's been longer than that already.

Ought. A funny word that echoes in my brain and in my sleep and in my water-packed tuna on whole wheat (when what I really want is chocolate). Ought has even permeated my dinner! Where is that SAFE place where ought doesn't live?

I've got to run away and find that place.

And so, today, I did just that. I ran away. I became a famous trapeze artist and a dancer on the high wire. My costume (what little there was) was glittery and sparkly, but there was no safety net!

THERE WAS NO NET!

So I had to come home, because it wasn't safe out there. I plugged in the coffee pot again, threw in a load of laundry and picked up the pieces—just where I'd left them.

Today, I ran away and left the world of ought for a few minutes. And when I got back, the world was just the same, but I wasn't. I quit emphasizing ought and I quit worrying about worrying. Mostly, I quit trying not to hurt. I just decided to fly with the hurt, to eat the oat bran and the green, leafy vegetables *and* the chocolate. I also decided to live without the net and hope for the best.

I ran away today. And I quit oughting....

See you at the circus.

September Again

Ah, September, the beginning of the real New Year. I've never understood why the calendar-makers don't realize that September, not January, marks the beginning of every new year. Everyone remembers the smell of new crayons, the stiffness of new shoes and the pride of the new lunchbox.

Of course, lunchboxes aren't made of tin anymore; and my heroes, Popeye, Sky King and Captain Midnight are long gone. But I think the contents of these poly-something-or-other containers are pretty close to historic. Remember the peanut-butter-and-jelly that got squished together into something unrecognizable? Now they have yogurt raisins, pudding on a stick and mystery meat that isn't even meat!

Each September, we started over, inspired by our father's lecture on the hardships of when he was a boy and how far he had to walk to school through blinding blizzards and gale-force winds. Then came the lecture from Mom about how precious and wonderful and necessary an education is so you can grow up and become something ("better than your father," which was always said under her breath). We knew what they were really trying to say was, "Grow up, leave home and send money back to your beloved and aging parents!"

Each September, we received new pencils, a plastic ruler and advice. Most of that advice has long since faded from memory, but perhaps in September, as we mark the beginning of another year, a few survival tactics wouldn't hurt:

TIPS FOR SURVIVING THE FIRST YEAR OF FOREVER—AND BEYOND—OR FOR SURVIVING THE DEATH OF SOMEONE YOU LOVE—OR FOR LIVING THROUGH THE FIRST GRADE AGAIN!

- BE YOURSELF. It's too hard to be somebody else, and you probably can't remember who you said you were anyway.

- FIND ENOUGH COMPASSIONATE LISTENERS. You can talk more than one person can listen.

- PICK YOUR WORRIES. Give up just worrying about worrying.

- Don't assume others know what is happening. WEAR A SIGN: "I'm Bereaved." It's a good excuse for just about everything, and it will get you excused to use the bathroom without question!

- EXERCISE. Walk, jog, jump rope, fly a kite or a paper airplane. Watch someone else exercise. At least jog your memory.

57

- BUY SOMETHING. Treat yourself. It's Charge-card Therapy!

- DO NOT EAT ANYTHING in the cafeteria line that could be LABELED "MYSTERY MEAT." (Ice cream, chocolate and Oreos are always safe—they cannot be disguised as something healthy.)

- ALWAYS FOLLOW THE PERSON AT THE FRONT OF THE LINE. If everyone gets lost, it's his fault. Besides, a group of lost people gathered together aren't lost—they are where they are.

- FOLLOW THE RULES. If not, you get your name on the chalkboard, and everyone knows you aren't doing IT right; or you are taking too long to get over IT, and who knows how long IT should take, anyway? Grief takes far longer than anyone imagines.

- INSIST ON JOY EVERY DAY. Create your own magic, your own sandwich, your own rules and your own survival tactics. Walk in your own shoes, carry your own pencil box and never, never, never loan your lunchbox or your grief to anyone else. They won't take care of it as well as you can.

September: new beginnings marked by painful passages from the light of Summer to the finality of Fall. It isn't the end of anything, only the beginning of a new beginning. Start now to recognize and become the person you already are!

Look both ways before crossing, and hold hands. Carry an umbrella, wear clean underwear and hang on tight....

Forever is just beginning.

"HIHOWYADOIN?"

Smile-On-A-Stick

It's Fall again, and the leaves are beginning to change. I wonder how they know when to turn and if they know beforehand what color they are going to become? Do they get to pick their colors? Do leaves know they are destined to grow, turn and fall?

Do they know they will become a source of great joy to children who will jump into huge piles of them or of great fatigue to those adults who have to rake them up again? Do leaves care? Does anyone ever stop to ask the leaves what they are feeling or how they are doing? Have you ever stopped and asked a maple leaf how it's doing?

Of course not. Yet, we are asked every day how we are doing. I sometimes feel like I should be the weatherman (excuse me, weather person) who posts weather warnings: whether you should talk to me today or not.

Everyone wants to know how I am doing; not what I am doing, but how I am doing. Every place I go, there are kindly faces asking me, "HOW ARE YOU DOING TODAY?" Did they ever ask me before? Well, actually, yes. Traditionally, everyone asks, "How are you doing?" We greet each other with "Hi" or "Hello," and then we follow immediately with a "How are you doing?" question, delivered at lightning speed, which is matched only by the pace of our exiting feet! We don't expect an answer to our question, so we don't wait for any kind of response. The actual greeting consists of "HIHOWYADOIN?" but no one really wants to know.

Do we ask dogs how they are doing? Do we stop and query the yard? (Mine would simply gasp for water.) Do we engage in conversation with the wind or the moon? All these things change, too, but we are the only ones whose daily transformation into something different is monitored and recorded by the grim nods of understanding heads.

Fall is a time of change—for all of us. Half the world begins its journey into Winter's sleep, while the other half stretches awake into Spring. Do we ever ask the world how it's doing?

I think the reason no one wants to know is that we are all afraid that someone might not be doing very well, and then what are we to do or say or think or feel? Gads!

To combat the "Hihowyadoin?" syndrome, I have developed an answer that can be delivered faster than the fleetest foot. I believe everyone, bereaved or not, who has ever been patted on the back, suffered acne or lost their most important possession (a #2 lead pencil at the S.A.T. site) will find this helpful.

I have developed a Smile-On-A-Stick. It can be carried at all times and used whenever that dreaded "Hihowyadoin?" question arrives. We can whisk it out, display it across our face and mutter "Fine, thanks," in any tone of voice that suits our current mood.

I have discovered that Smile-On-A-Stick satisfies the curiosity of even the most dedicated "Hihowyadoin?" mutterer, and we can both go about our day feeling responsible, compassionate and sensitive. It's cheap to make and costs far less than psychotherapy (which I often recommend for the friends of the bereaved).

It won't cure anything and it won't stop the leaves from falling or the snow from burying the driveway. It won't fix the leaky faucet or cure a broken heart. But Smile-On-A-Stick can speak a thousand words for those who walk slowly enough to hear the answer and it becomes the mask for those who need to have us wear one.

"Hihowyadoin?"

"I'm fine, thanks." I have been ever since I made my own Smile-On-A-Stick. It's my sense of perspective, my sense of humor, my attempt at turning the falling leaves into a playful pile in which to jump instead of a chore done alone now....

Don't ever be without one. Pass them around at your next office meeting. You don't have to be bereaved to need one. "Hihowyadoin?" can strike anywhere, and now we have the answer for which everyone has been waiting. The ready-made smile that says to those who only see superficially, "I'm fine"; but to those who both see and listen, it says, "I'm struggling, hurt, angry, tired, lonely, confused, but not dead! I think I'll make it, thanks."

Do leaves worry about what others think when they cascade into piles on the lawn? Probably not, but if you see a tiny Smile-On-A-Stick in that pile of leaves— maybe we're not the only ones who need a listening heart!

Light a Candle for Love

It doesn't snow in Louisiana. I can see palm trees from my window, and our boat is gently bobbing at the dock in my backyard. There is a snow shovel in the garage (left over from Missouri), but I don't think I'll be using it this year. It doesn't snow in Louisiana.

How can you have Winter if it doesn't snow? I'm out mowing my lawn, and the rest of the world is shoveling snow. How can you have holidays in weather like this?!

I miss the snow. The preseason holiday hoopla in the stores seems a bit silly when the temperature is above 90 degrees Fahrenheit. But, whether we're ready or not, it's TIME.

It's time to think about decorating the yard for the holidays. What should I put up this year? We're new in the neighborhood and we want to make a good impression. Does everyone string colored lights around their boat docks? Should we decorate the palm trees with those giant inflatable ornaments? Should we go electric this year, or will a single candle in the window do? I guess I could toss some tinsel over the air conditioner, but it won't be the same. It never is . . . is it?

It's hard to know just what to do when you're new. Being new in the neighborhood is a lot like being new in grief. You're not quite sure why you're here and you can't find anything.

You know you're missing something, and nothing seems to fit in its place anymore. Your ears and eyes are too filled with "goodbye" to begin to say, "hello." It's a strange time, made even stranger by the fact that it isn't even going to snow!

Everyone else is busy decorating their yard and their boat dock, but so far mine remains plain and bare. I thought about putting up glowing plastic penguins and setting Santa up in the front yard, but it all seems so out of place here in the land of no snow. Maybe we'll just forget it this year.

Maybe you've decided to leave your house and yard bare this year, too. Not because you moved to the swamp, but because nothing seems quite right this season—in your house or your heart. Can you ever be happy again? Will the sights and sounds of the holiday season ever touch you again? Will the emptiness always be this big?

No.

Nothing stays the same, not even grief. Just as I am busy unpacking my gypsy bag in another new place; you, too, are trying to figure out where to put things this year—in a new you. It's hard to find new places to stash the old memories. And besides, those memories hurt! They hurt too much to put them away and they hurt too much to keep them out. How are you going to make it through the holidays?

Be patient with yourself this holiday season. If you can't decorate the yard, then decorate the house. If the house seems too big to tackle, then decorate a room, a corner, a table. But whatever you do, don't lose the holidays completely.

It may not snow in Louisiana, but I'm going to have pink flamingos in the front yard holding a giant greeting card. It's not the same, but it is something. I refuse to lose the joy of holidays past and the anticipation of holidays future just because....

I may not get any cookies baked this year, or the cards written, but you'll see those pink flamingos out in front and you'll see a tiny candle in the window.

No matter how shattered your life, how fragmented your dreams, there must be light somewhere. There must be HOPE somewhere, too. It must be snowing someplace, even if I'm not there.

As long as I know it's Winter somewhere, as long as I know there is joy someplace, then I know it will come to me again (and to you as well!). We just have to hang on tight and believe.

Believe in whatever you choose, but at least light a candle this holiday season, remember the pink flamingos in my yard (flashing out a "Happy Holidays" greeting) and remember the joy that used to light your own heart.

Light a candle for hope and for remembrance. No matter where you are or which holiday it is for you, light a candle for love. It is the greatest light of all!

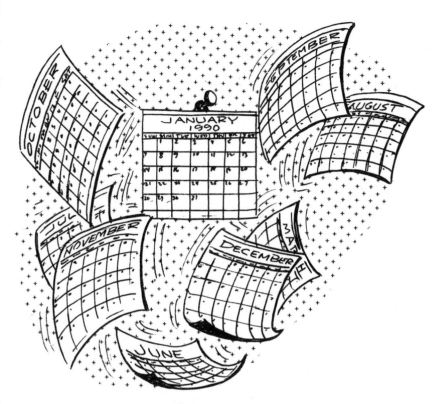

Am I Making Progress?

January is a month for reflection. Ice ponds reflect the leaden sky, and the heart reflects the emptiness of a frozen spirit. When will we begin to thaw? When will we feel like we're making some progress in this place of icicles and cold sheets, sunless days and long, empty nights? Will we ever be happy again? Will I ever be me again?

January is also the month for making promises, commitments and resolutions (which are fancy promises). We begin our new year with high hopes, strong wills and long lists of things that will be different this year. To celebrate my commitment to a new me, I bought a jogging suit, expensive shoes and a digital watch—complete with timer, pulse meter and an M & M candy dispenser. (You've got to have some motivation!) THIS YEAR WILL BE DIFFERENT!

As we spend time looking back over the road we've traveled, sometimes we wonder if we have made any progress at all. In the beginning, we misplaced car keys, checkbooks, toothbrushes, relatives and important stuff like the TV Guide.

We had to begin making lists of everything. We simply couldn't remember anything. I couldn't remember my address, Social Security number, zip code or my mother-in-law's birthday. (I never could remember that.) I even started making lists of my lists! I knew I was going to be OK when I first discovered I could remember that I had made a list.

You know you're making progress when you can coordinate an entire outfit again. Shoes, belts, ties, purses—even sweaters and jackets—often got left, simply because when we were hurting so terribly we couldn't think about what to wear. Many of us didn't even know that the panty hose were on backwards or that the tie was crooked. If you are wearing matched shoes right now, then you are making progress.

You're making progress if you no longer choke back tears when you say your loved one's name. When you can walk down the cereal aisle in the supermarket and not dissolve into tears, progress is being made. When you can enjoy baking his or her favorite cookies or pie or cake again, you are on your way.

When you again can set the pictures out and wander through the scrapbooks—letting the smiles peek through the tears—hope is returning. When, for the most part, memories bring comfort and warmth instead of emptiness and pain, January grows shorter. When you begin to understand that putting away your loved one's things does NOT mean putting him or her out of your life, your step becomes lighter.

Progress occurs when you completely understand that though your loved one died, the love you shared can never be destroyed. Hope begins to return when you can hear laughter again—and some of that laughter is your own.

Recovery is possible once we have given up unrealistic hopes for a lost future, grieved for that loss and moved beyond. Perhaps it is not so much a matter of saying goodbye to my loved one as it is of saying farewell to the old me and to the life we shared.

Making progress through grief doesn't mean that we no longer miss our loved ones. They will be a part of our lives forever, but their roles in our lives have changed. Our lifestyles and habits now reflect a different family landscape.

As we look back, it is amazing to see how the life fabric is no longer a gaping hole, torn apart. It's mended now with tiny stitches (perhaps a bit lumpy, like lots of us), patched with time, effort and love. Old threads and new threads have been rewoven and blended into a pattern not quite the same as we had originally planned. It is a tapestry of love given and received, love remembered and shared.

Life can become good and whole and complete once again; not as we try to fill up the empty spaces left by loved ones no longer within hug's reach, but when we realize that love creates new spaces in the heart, expands the spirit and deepens the joy of simply being alive.

As the Winter of our grief turns into Spring, the renewed energy and love we feel becomes a memorial to our loved ones. Our tributes are not in the grave markers we decorate, not in the books we write, not in the speeches we give. They are in the love we share and pass on.

You know you are making progress when all of this begins to make some sense. (Save this chapter to read later!) When your shoes match and your car keys are found and the list of lists grows shorter, then you are making progress. Then laughter can return and with that magical sound comes the healing of the hurt and the shedding of the Band-Aid, because the heart is learning to sing again.

January . . . the month to check our progress, to make new commitments and to start jogging.

Hope springs eternal!

Candy Hearts

I've always wanted to write the messages that come on those little candy hearts. I think I could do a better job than the writing genius who imprints "I LUV U" or "Cutie Pie" on those pastel teeth-breakers.

Because just about everyone gets those little candies at Valentine's Day (and if you have an economical mother, you might also get them at Easter), I'd like to see their messages have some meaning.

We could imprint some safety tips on them, like "Unplug The Iron When You're Finished," or "A Full Tank Of Gas Will Get You Farther." And don't forget, "Strangers ARE."

Diet tips could also be valuable on those hearts: "Consumption Of This Candy Heart Will Require Twenty-Nine-And-One-Half Minutes Of Incredibly Difficult Jogging To Burn Off The Caloric Content."

Or, "Don't Forget FIBER." Then there's my personal favorite, "A Moment On The Lips, A Lifetime On The Hips."

Maybe we should use those tiny morsels to warn consumers about things: "Blue Light Specials May Not Be!" Or, "Life Is Dangerous: Proceed With Caution."

Other safety tips would be good, too: "Protect Your Heart: It Could Break," or, "Love Can Be Life-Threatening." Maybe we could write "Tear Zone: Life Jacket Required."

It's hard to catch the Valentine spirit when you're still exhausted from the holiday rush and the January deep-freeze. The sight of red-velvet cupids and frothy lace can send an "I think I might make it" survivor right back to the closet—in search of a place where candy hearts don't exist.

It doesn't seem fair now to have to endure the messages of "I LUV U" and "Mine" and "Forever Yours." Forever??? Forever was shorter than I had planned! The fancy card or the sticky paste Valentine won't be for me this year.

Yes, I've always wanted to pen the little messages on those little candy hearts. I know I could do a better job than the dreamer who thought up "I LUV U!" I'd tell the world to "Watch Out! Be Careful! Stop! Look! Listen!" And I wouldn't make those candy hearts pastel colored either. There would just be black hearts, to suit the real world, because it seems like there are more empty hearts than red ones.

Why can't the world realize that Valentine's Day is just a meaningless, silly ritual that will only cause heartache and pain? Why can't they know that in my world it's not Valentine's Day this year? Why didn't the rest of the world stop when mine did??? Why?!!!

Why?

Because, just as there are hearts like ours that are aching and empty, there are also hearts that are waiting to be filled, hearts waiting to be repaired, hearts waiting to be found.

Hearts are everywhere, in all sizes and shapes and with all kinds of needs. I have one, too. And it's working OK, but it took another heart to fill my life to overflowing. It took another heart to make the flowers blossom and the birds sing. It took another heart to set my world aglow.

As long as the shelves keep filling with cartoon Valentines, Batman greeting cards, heart-shaped lollipops, boxes of red cherries and an endless assortment of chocolate everything, somebody must know something! Somebody must be loving somewhere. Somebody must like those chalky-tasting candy hearts.

I remember that I used to. I bought it all: something for everyone and everything for someone, for one extra-special heart.

That's gone now, but the hearts still keep coming. The world is filled with the sounds of billions of hearts beating. Some are empty, some are hurting, some are crying, some are singing; but they are all beating and singing a lifetime story.

Mine still beats, too. A little slower, maybe. A little more painfully sometimes, but I "ain't dead yet," even though I suppose I should tell you there are/were days....

But Valentine's Day keeps coming, because love isn't something to be packed away, buried or kept hidden. Maybe love can't solve all the problems or heal all the hurts, but without it, nothing will work. A billion-plus hearts are telling you and me this season that even though death has come, love didn't die!

So eat the candy hearts and jog away the silly calories, but rest secure in the LOVE that once sent your heart flying. That love is still there! Search for it; find it; remember it.

And go ahead, buy the candy heart that says, "I LUV U," because I DO!

Anger

The whole world was picking on me today. EVERY SINGLE traffic light in the entire world was red, just for me, today! Everybody else had a green light, but not me. Oh, no! I got 281 red lights today! Not even a yellow, caution light—just red ones. Just for me.

The faucet dripped ALL night, too. I was the only one who heard it, but it dripped all right! Just for me. They ran out of Creamed Broccoli On Toast Points at my favorite restaurant, and the mailman had mail for everyone in the house, except me!

I got three hang-up phone calls on the answering machine and one I wished had hung up. My shoelace broke at the two-mile marker, and I had to walk home. Since I had forgotten my key, I had to wait for my four-mile-husband to come back. I sat on the curb and waited and got two mosquito bites....

The clock was ticking at me all morning, and the typewriter wouldn't spell right. I know I heard the news-

71

caster snicker at me when I turned on the television, and the pizza delivery person couldn't find our house. Besides all that, it snowed in New Orleans over Christmas while we went home to the mountains— where it didn't snow at all!

At the supermarket, I had only three items in my basket and the lady in front of me had thirteen (everyone knows there are *twelve* eggs in that carton). Did she think we were all stupid?!

I picked the shortest line at the bank, too, and I could have become a grandmother before I got to the window. Today, even the flowers bloomed too loudly. Life is against me; it's just NOT FAIR!

I want to shake my fist at something. I want to yell and scream and kick and bite. I do! I want to bite someone! And I don't mean a little love nibble either. I mean a great big CHOMP! I'm mad, and nobody even notices that. They all think I'm doing "fine," but then all the lights didn't turn red just for them today, either.

Now I'm mad. No . . . I'm angry. Mad isn't enough of a word. I'm really enraged. I'm tired of life picking on me. Why can't it pick on somebody else— someone stronger, someone nicer, someone less tired than I? LEAVE ME ALONE! I don't want to answer the phone or read the mail or hurt anymore. Just leave me alone.

Anger is one of those uncomfortable feelings that most adults believe they aren't supposed to have. By the time we're old enough to "act our age," we usually do. We learn early not to act on our feelings, especially the angry ones. You can't even attend kindergarten if you're a "biter." So, we learn quickly not to bite people who deserve a good chomp or anger will make us socially unacceptable. Grief isn't socially acceptable either and that makes me even madder! But I've got it, and so do you.

With fists upheld, we rage against the sky. "IT'S NOT FAIR!" we shriek. And it's not.

Just because I learned not to bite people doesn't mean I don't want to sometimes. Each of us has a list of people we know who deserve to be bitten. But we don't do it. Instead, we carry that anger around until it becomes a madness that can send us into a rage simply because the sounds of life continue—just at the time when we think our own life has (or should have) ended.

I guess life isn't really picking on me, but it sure seems that way sometimes. If only I could retrain my thoughts to accept the occasional delays and side-tracks and dead ends and empty spaces. If only I could learn not to be destroyed by those angry feelings, but to acknowledge how much they hurt me, inconvenience me, stumble me, but not consume me. Surely I must be more than just a mass of anger....

But just knowing it's all right to feel anger does not help alleviate my inner storms. I carry a brick with me at all times. I never know when I might need one, so it's wise to keep one handy. Sometimes just picking up the brick helps. Just caressing it, feeling it, imagining where it's going to land . . . sometimes that helps dispel the anger that boils inside me. It also delivers a pretty clear anger-message to those around me. Not many people can guess what I might do when I pick up my brick.

And when just picking up the brick isn't enough, I throw it. For in the throwing—the actual physical tossing of the brick—anger is released. My brick happens to be a foam-rubber "Nerf" brick, because I don't really want to hurt anyone or anything. But sometimes I surely do want to throw a brick!

It doesn't do any good to stand in the living room and stomp my foot and say, "Darn! I'm angry about being alone or hurt or tired or picked on." That just increases my frustration, which increases my helpless-ness, which increases my anger. Throwing a brick re-leases the intensity of the emotion that we mature, grown-up, responsible adults refrain from experienc-ing. I recommend that you get a brick. Now.

Workbench therapy is also a positive way to re-lease anger. Pounding a piece of wood is wonderfully

73

therapeutic, but I suggest you do not pound anything that is attached to a building or to body parts.

I use a small, plastic hammer with a squeaker inside. Every time I slam the hammer against the wood, it takes the full force of my anger and turns it into a high-pitched "eeekkk." Every time I do that, I've allowed myself the anger, and it has turned into something else, something less harmful than rage.

It's better than drinking. It's better than eating an entire display case of chocolate doughnuts and it's safer than staying angry. Sometimes I yell in the backyard. I also talk with various characters in thin air, giving them suggestions as to what they can do with certain things. No one has to hear for me to release the rage. Occasionally, I talk to people who are driving in the other lane. Sometimes I even wave. Sometimes they wave back—with their fingers.

Sometimes I have to drag out my old and battered box of garage-sale "china" and troop into the backyard where I have spread newspapers up against the side of the garage or fence. There, whenever I need to, I can select the size plate or cup or (if it's been a really bad day) platter, and slam it against the wall— watching my anger shatter into a million pieces of cheap porcelain and crockery.

Ridiculous? I suppose.

Immature? Definitely.

But maybe that's what we hurting and grieving folks need to be once in awhile. Maybe we need to acknowledge our pain and our hurt and our rage against the unfairness of it all. We did everything right we could possibly do. We ate the spinach, we cleaned our rooms, we put money in the collection plate and we still got *THIS*. It still didn't work!

Sometimes the anger just spills out as part of the grieving process. But because we learned early that anger and rage are not socially acceptable, we learned to bury those emotions and to deny the inner fires.

Maybe I'll have to learn that it's all right to be angry; that this is not the journey I had planned for myself or for my loved ones; this is not what I expected! But it does appear to be what I got! And anger is a powerful response to being surprised.

It's only a red light. I've got to remember that. Maybe I'll have to change my vision a bit. Maybe I'll have to learn to see that anger isn't something awful, but actually something normal and natural—a part of the grieving process.

So, go ahead and figure out some personally nondestructive technique to release the full intensity of your natural anger. Dream up some ridiculous way to allow yourself to acknowledge the full strength of your emotions and then release those emotions in ways that will not hurt you or anyone else.

Maybe you will decide to throw a foam brick or yell in the backyard at midnight or chop wood or knead dough or dig fence-post holes, but whatever you choose, use it! Return to the land of being four years old, when you knew just who to bite and how. Find a way to address that anger; and do it now, before it harms you and destroys your path to the other side of grief.

Red lights do pick on certain people. The trick is not to look like one of those people! When you figure that out, please write. I'll probably still be right here—stuck at a red light.

Mother. . . Love in a Single Word

There are certain rules for being a mother. The trouble is no one ever tells us these rules until it's too late. If they had known about the "RULES OF MOTHERHOOD," few moms ever would have ventured forth into Gerber-land. It was easier just being a wife. In fact, it was probably easier being single . . . but no one told us about that either!

To celebrate Mother's Day this year, I thought it would be appropriate to quickly review some of the more important rules of motherhood so you can evaluate yourself and/or your mother. Even if you aren't a mother, somebody you know is; and, by the way, you wouldn't be reading this if it weren't for your mother.

The first and most important rule of motherhood is, "It's Mother's fault." No matter what has happened or is about to happen or will happen some time in the future, it is always Mother's fault. I realized this several years ago when I was attending a psychology seminar about guilt.

The more I listened to the presenters, the more I realized the source of guilt in my life was my mother. I reasoned that if my mother (and father) had not been doing whatever they were doing so many years ago, I would not have been born. Therefore, everything that has happened in my life has actually been caused by their actions.

I called my mom that evening and told her that I just wanted to get one thing straight: It was her fault! I went on to explain my theory, and she hung up. Rule Number Two for mothers is, "Never listen to your children after they have attended a psychological seminar on guilt."

There are other rules for mothers, too. Some of them are easy, such as, "Always be prepared to feed twelve (with only fifteen seconds notice)" and, "It is a mother's responsibility not only to purchase the toilet paper, but to replace the empty roll in the bathroom as well." Apparently no one else is capable of installing a new roll of toilet paper.

Mothers should be able to do the laundry, the ironing, bake four-dozen cupcakes for the Cub Scout meeting and hem a prom dress—all while suffering from a migraine. Mothers are not allowed to become sick, injured or otherwise occupied. Vacations are for other family members, though when on vacation (translated: work in a strange place with no running water, no refrigeration and no microwave), mothers may be allowed to substitute pizza for the traditional Sunday chicken dinner.

Rules of behavior for mothers are subtle. Mothers should protect their young, but from a distance. Mothers of children older than nine should remain at least one block behind their children at all times. Names should be changed before arriving at the PTA meeting, and no mother ever is allowed to identify her-self as belonging to a teenager (except when posting bail or paying credit card bills). Mothers are also not allowed to cry, comment, speak or burp in public. Most mothers should not wear shorts at any time.

Meals are to be served "whenever," and it is not acceptable for a mother to inquire about the whereabouts of any family member. Mothers, however, must post their schedules on the refrigerator alongside the instructions for locating the nearest mother-substitute (usually grandmother) in case of an emergency. Brownies are to be available at all times; and when playing Monopoly, mothers should not acquire all utilities or put more than one hotel on Park Place.

Mothers are to be available twenty-four hours a day for counseling, dispensing of Band-Aids and ironing clothes. Mothers should not sleep, yawn, appear bored, confused or too knowledgeable. Vacuum cleaners are a mother's best friend, and mothers should never use the phone after school or in the evenings. Mothers should not work outside the home except in the garden. Mothers should be seen and not heard.

Mothers should love their children unconditionally, even when posting bail or arranging for adoption of the boa constrictor that "got a little too big."

Gift-giving is a mother's joy and obligation, but a mother also should be appreciative of the handmade card received two weeks after her birthday. Mothers over age forty should not be.

Vegetables belong to mothers. Only mothers could get excited over rutabagas, squash and broccoli. Mothers must serve nutritious meals that do not contain fiber or anything green. Mothers may eat anything on their children's plates that resembles "healthful," but the Twinkies are for kids only. Mothers must share their candy, but they may not nibble the ears off the chocolate bunny. Mothers must hide the eggs and then remember where they are—especially the real ones!

Homework is a mother's speciality. She should be able to do ninth-grade algebra, diagram sentences and build a working model of a volcano while feeding the baby, coordinating the carpool and entertaining guests. Mothers must help sell enough Girl Scout cookies, band candy and magazine subscriptions to earn their children free weeks at camp, assorted uniform parts and a stuffed Panda bear. Mothers will not have any friends left by the time their children graduate from junior high.

Mothers must be brave and must not follow their newly licensed teen driver everywhere. Mothers must be strong, humble, quiet, always available and loving at all times.

Mothers experience heartache and joy, satisfaction and disappointment, but they must never be tired or discouraged. They are the family cheerleaders and fire-builders. They keep the morale high and the door open. They must have built-in clocks, all-seeing eyes, arms as wide as the world and hearts with endless space—they can always find room for one more of anything.

A mother is the reason we are. Without a mother, the world would starve and weep uncomforted. Without mothers, we would grow cold and weary and be lost. Mothers know where we have been, where we are and where we are going. They have dreams for their children; and they know their offspring will dance across paths they can only imagine. They stand straight against the wind and loan their sweaters to the less-fortunate.

All mothers loved once, and once all mothers were loved— even if only for a brief moment. It was in that moment that life was created and love was given a name: yours.

Thank you, Mother, for being the cause of my life and the source of my own ability to love. I shall not spoil the fun. The rules of motherhood will remain a secret for my own daughter to discover. Mothers know that if everyone knew the rules there would be no mothers and joy, as we know it, would not exist.

Mother: the friend of vegetables and children, the companion of Man, the source of everything.

Mother . . . love in a single word.

Men!

Next time around, I think I'm going to come back as a man. Life seems less complicated for them! They don't worry about underwear, ring-around-the-collar, carpool schedules or menu planning. Men don't worry about matching shoes and purse, hem lines or the life span of pantyhose. I'm not sure they worry about anything (nothing important that is).

Of course, life always looks greener on the other side of the fence, just as my neighbor's yard always looks better than mine—no matter where I live!

Nevertheless, I am convinced that life as a man would not be all bad. Men are fairly simple in their requests about life: good meal, plenty of peanuts, an uninterrupted Sunday afternoon for football, clean shirts and the companionship of a faithful dog. A wife and children are optional.

Men are also fairly simple in their relationships and in their demands of others. They seek instant gratification, require immediate obedience of their commands and offer no obligations. Their range of emotions is also uncomplicated: anger, boredom, laughter and sleep. It is not too difficult to figure men out—it is a bit more difficult to live with (or without) them!

Men may look simple on the outside, but I have discovered that on the inside they are a complicated mixture of little boy, towering giant, macho-nacho and small, furry animal. Men are not allowed to show any of these internal features to the outside world; but if you have a man in your life, you have probably seen at least the little boy and the macho-nacho sides of your man.

The little boy who resides within is left over from when you were not the woman in his life (unless you are his mother). Within his being, a man keeps his mother in a very sacred place where she becomes more and more wonderful the longer they are apart. The little boy part of a man still believes that the dirty clothes magically find their way into the hamper, that tapioca pudding should be a part of every meal and that he will be loved unconditionally. The macho-nacho character appears during football—or any other sports season—and he is characterized by a rise in voice level when cheering or booing the TV and when announcing frequent requests for more of whatever you just ran out of.

The furry-little-animal side of men rarely is seen, but can often be felt during an unexpected cuddle or when he is sometimes caught gazing at his offspring while they are romping in the Spring grass. There is something about the eyes that gives this creature away. They become gentle and almost misty. There is a softening of those enormous hands whenever this sometimes giant examines the wonders of his child's first crayon drawing.

Tears are also a part of the furry-little-animal side of man. They are always there, but they are seldom seen on the outside. Though this manifestation of man doesn't appear often, make no mistake, it is there.

The towering-giant side of man is the one he would most often like to have us see. It is the strong, capable, protective side that tells the world he always knows where the car keys are, has all the bills paid in full and on time, is in control of everything he can see and touch and commands respect and obedience by his very presence. Many men spend a lot of time hiding behind the towering-giant part of themselves—probably because that's what we expect of them.

But when I come back as a man next time, it is the ability to look at things and see nothing that I am hoping to gain. I want to be able to look at a living room full of newspapers, empty cans and Twinkie wrappers and see nothing out of place.

I want to be able to stand tall and look innocent, even puzzled, when confronted with the empty ice-cream carton. I want to not look guilty all the time.

I want to be more tired than "they" are. Just once, I want to be sicker than "they" are. I want to sleep later than "they" do because "I work." I want to be served and have my slippers waiting.

I want the kids to obey me. I want to go to my closet and put on the same shirt, slacks and tie that I have worn for twenty years and walk out of the house oblivious to the stares and comments of neighbors and children!

Yes, next time I am coming back as a man!

Actually, I'm not sure I want to come back at all next time around. Maybe there isn't another time around. Maybe this is it. Maybe it isn't any greener over there than it is here. Maybe it just looks that way. Maybe I should stop asking MAN to be the things I want him to be. Maybe I should just figure out what he is and love that. Maybe I should stop expecting him to be a combination of laughter, tears, joy, fear, anger, sadness, guilt and love....

Men are different than women, but we don't always act like we know that. We expect our men to be what we need them to be. We demand that they be what we cannot be, are not prepared to be and don't want to be.

If we are strong, we want someone to recognize that. If we are tired, we don't want someone else to flop on the couch first. When we are sick, we don't want someone else to be sick first.

I want someone else to answer the call for "night water," someone else to take the kids to the dentist. I want someone else to be "on guard" all the time—just for a little while, anyway. I want the freedom we give our men, but I don't want all the restrictions we place on them!

No matter what kind of experience we have had with men, we want them to be different: more compassionate, stronger, smarter (but not too much . . .), better looking, gentler, kinder, richer (especially richer!), more understanding and able to leap tall buildings with a single bound and change in phone booths whenever the occasion arises.

We want to be comforted without having to tell him, and we want to be showered with gifts of the heart at the exact moment we hit rock bottom. In short, we'd like to have it all!

Men: We women have not created an easy existence for you. Perhaps that is because life simply isn't very easy on either side of the gender-fence.

I guess it all has to do with expectations. I want you to know exactly what I need and when I need it— even when I can't figure that out. I want you to understand me, be like me, grieve like me, recover like me, hurt like me, live like me . . . and most of all, LIKE me!

But, thanks for being the other side. It is always good to have another fence to climb, another yard to compare with mine, another field to dream upon. Men, you are the answer to our prayers! (You may not be exactly what we prayed for, but you do appear to be the answer....)

Thanks for being there, even if I don't understand why you are over there and I'm over here. I guess we can all cope and manage alone, but a little company along the way makes the journey less painful. And, at least it's never boring!

Rose-colored Glasses

There are some days when nothing helps. Silent pain echoes across the heart, leaving tear stains and shattered dreams. It hurts to move, to think, to breathe. It even hurts to be. On those days, when memories burn scars deep into the soul, there seems little relief.

All the coping tricks we have tried in the past seem to fail us, and we are left with a pain so deep that we fear we will be consumed by it. We firmly believe that we shall never again find hope or joy in this world. Our own death often seems the only escape.

That despair comes at the bottom of the valley. We have all stumbled across those treacherous rocks—many of us more than once. Just as we begin to think that we might survive, something tumbles us back into the darkness, and we are sure we have drowned.

What then? It is as if we are left without our dreams or our memories. Existence has become a void, filled with nothingness— not even hurt. On those days, we cannot even feel our pain. We come to know that we can never return to the Land of Make-believe where Humpty Dumpty is put back together without a trace of the jagged edges where he broke into a million pieces and where everything lives happily ever after.

Those are the days when we must "put on" our rose-colored glasses and learn to "see" in new ways. I always carry my rose-colored glasses with me because I never know when such a day is going to happen.

My special glasses give a rosy hue to even the most dismal of views; but more important, people look at me differently. Maybe they see me differently because I see things in a new way.

Just putting on my rose-colored glasses gives me a lift. I know that whatever I am looking at or feeling hasn't really changed. I have changed! Whenever I have dared to laugh in the face of pain, the pain didn't change or go away. I simply changed the way I saw the pain or the emptiness or the hurt of grief.

Rose-colored glasses are simply a dramatic (and perhaps a little silly) change in perspective. But what's wrong with being silly sometimes? If I can catch my breath and gain a few seconds of relief from the emptiness of my grief, then they have created a miracle for me.

Wearing rose-colored glasses isn't denying anything. Rather, it is claiming it all. It is searching for joy and light and love, even in the darkest of corners. Love is the reason we hurt, but on those days when all we can see is the hurt, then we fear we may be losing the love.

Life does become good and warm and loving once again, but only when we have learned to trust enough to move through the hurt and to claim even that which hurts so terribly. It is a part of us, and as such cannot be ignored or abandoned.

Looking at the world through rose-colored glasses isn't being a Pollyanna, it's being real in the most honest sense. It is an attempt to both accept and live what is instead of turning it all away and denying that love ever existed.

If you ever laughed with your loved one, you have already worn rose-colored glasses. Don't forget them now. They helped you conquer mountains before and they will help you to see the other side of grief, someday.

Don't wait for joy to come to you . . . go find it. Search for it, insist on it every day. Wearing rose-colored glasses is a change in perspective; nothing more, nothing less. It is not a choice between pain or no pain, but how we manage the pain we feel.

The trick to those days is learning to live with what you got instead of wishing something else had happened. As you pick your next step through the valley, remember that the rocks are everywhere, but so is the path!

Don't let death rob you of your heart spaces . . . the place where your loved one lives. Don't let death dominate the Spring places in your heart. Don't let death rob you of your rose-colored glasses.

Also from Big A and Company

"**A**t last . . . a moving story now told . . . of a BIG SISTER'S love for her little brother and of a Mum and Dad who cared and shared."

A sensitive, caring journal of a hurting child trying to understand death. Alicia Sims, author, asks and answers "WHO AM I NOW that a loved one has died?" Written by a child for other children, it describes in a child's language, the path through pain to healing and hope. An excellent resource for young children and a wonderful program for a children's support group.

Big A and Company
Post Office Box 92032
Albuquerque, NM 87199

Please send me the quantity of books I have listed below. I am enclosing my check or money order for $_____ which includes shipping charges.

Book Title	Qnty	Price	TOTAL
AM I STILL A SISTER	____	$5.00	____
Why Are the Casseroles Always Tuna?	____	$9.95	____
Shipping Charges (see chart below)			____

$2 for first book
$1 for each additional book.

> Quantity Discounts
> Available

Name _____

Address_____

City _____ State _____ Zip _____

Phone _____